WIL

jB Dal
   Green. C
      Dalton gang $15.95

Wil08364

D0810131

jB Dal
   Green. C
      Dalton gang $15.95

Wil08364

DEMCO

Outlaws and Lawmen of the Wild West

THE DALTON GANG

Carl R. Green
❋ and ❋
William R. Sanford

ENSLOW PUBLISHERS, INC.

44 Fadem Road   P.O. Box 38
Box 699   Aldershot
Springfield, N.J. 07081   Hants GU12 6BP
                            U.K.

Library of Congress Cataloging-in-Publication Data

Green, Carl R.
    The Dalton gang / Carl R. Green and William R. Sanford.
        p.   cm. — (Outlaws and lawmen of the wild west)
    Includes bibliographical references (p.) and index.
    ISBN 0-89490-588-0
    1. Dalton family—Juvenile literature. 2. Outlaws—West (U.S.)—
Biography—Juvenile literature. 3. Frontier and pioneer life—West
(U.S.)—Juvenile literature. 4. West (U.S.)—Biography—Juvenile
literature. [1. Robbers and outlaws. 2. Southwest, New—
History—1848-] I. Sanford, William R. (William Reynolds), 1927- .
II. Title. III. Series: Green, Carl R. Outlaws and lawmen of
the wild west.
F595.G84 1995
978'.02'0922—dc20
[B]   94-32509
                                          CIP
                                          AC

Printed in the United States of America

10 9 8 7 6 5 4 3 2 1

Illustration Credits: Carl R. Green and William R. Sanford, pp. 24, 36; Western History Collections, University of Oklahoma Library, pp. 11, 14, 15, 16, 25, 27, 33, 40, 42.

Cover Illustration: Michael David Biegel

CONTENTS

AUTHORS' NOTE

This book tells the true story of four outlaw brothers—Grat, Bill, Bob, and Emmett Dalton. Following in the footsteps of their distant cousins, the Younger brothers, the Daltons robbed a number of banks and trains in the 1890s. During their lifetimes, their exploits were featured in newspapers, magazines, and dime novels. In more recent years, their story has been retold in films and on television. Some of the stories told about them have been made up, but others are true. To the best of the authors' knowledge, all of the events described in this book really happened.

1
"THEM DALTONS MADE THE KATY GIVE US SOME COAL"

Seven outlaws waited at the Dalton hideout near Oklahoma's Canadian River. The men were restless, ready for action. Gang leader Bob Dalton told them to be patient. On this September day in 1891 his gang was made up of his brother Emmett Dalton, Charlie Pierce, George "Bitter Creek" Newcomb, Bill Powers, Bill Doolin, and Dick Broadwell. All were hard men, handy with guns and horses.

At midday Bob's girlfriend rode into camp. Eugenia Moore had ridden two hundred miles to bring good news. As Bob grilled deer steaks, she described a train that would make a good target. The Katy, as everyone called the MK&T Express, would be carrying payroll money for the Lehigh Coal Company.[1] By sundown the gang had agreed to a plan. The water stop at Lillietta in eastern Oklahoma looked like a good spot.

The outlaws reached Lillietta just after dark on September 15. As they rode along the railroad track, they met an old man and his wife. The old man told them that they were looking for lumps of coal that sometimes fell from the Katy as it roared past.

"If you'll wait up the track a piece you might find some coal after the express goes through," Bob Dalton told the couple.[2]

Lillietta was closed down for the night. Only the

The windmills and water tanks that serviced the steam trains of the Old West towered above the prairie. The Dalton brothers chose Lillietta, Oklahoma, for one of their robberies because they knew the MK&T Express would stop at that station for water.

train station was open. The darkness suited the outlaws. If the station agent saw them, he might signal the train not to stop.

The outlaws heard four short whistle blasts as the Katy neared the station. The engineer was asking, "Is it safe to stop?" The men held their breath. Beside the track, a signal arm began to bob up and down. The agent had given the all-clear signal.

The gang struck as the train slowed to a crawl. Bob, with Bill Doolin beside him, climbed into the cab of the locomotive. The engineer took one look at their rifles and put on the brakes. The other four outlaws spread out along both sides of the tracks. As the train braked, a few passengers opened their windows and leaned out. When the heads appeared the outlaws standing guard fired warning shots in the air. The heads vanished back inside the train.

Bill Powers ran to the express car. Bob Dalton and Doolin were close behind. When the clerk refused to open up, Powers splintered the door with a warning shot. Then he yelled that they were prepared to use dynamite. The threat broke the clerk's nerve. The door slid open. Bob climbed in and held out a sack. The clerk filled it with greenbacks, silver dollars, and bonds.

Minutes later the outlaws were back on the station platform. The sight of the bulging sack brought an angry buzz from the passengers. A few armed men started to climb down from the coaches. Doolin mounted his horse and charged the length of the train, firing as he rode. The passengers piled back onto the train.

Bob told the engineer to "get going." As he did so, he pointed down the track. "When you get down by the siding light yonder, you slow down and have the fireman heave off a few shovels of coal," he ordered.[3]

The seven outlaws galloped into the night. The sack, stuffed with $19,000, lay across Doolin's saddle horn. The job done, the men laughed at the thought of the old couple picking up coal. Perhaps they would tell their friends, "Them Daltons made the Katy give us some coal when they held up the express!"[4] The legend of the Dalton gang was growing fast.

2
GROWING UP IN A TIME OF TROUBLES

James Lewis Dalton, Jr., married Adeline Younger in 1851. The 200-pound farmer, stockman, and part-time saloonkeeper was thirty-six. His red-haired wife was sixteen. Despite her youth, Adeline had strong views about right and wrong. She knew her father's cousins, the outlaw Younger brothers, had gone bad. That would not happen in her family if she could help it.

Adeline told Lewis she did not approve of his saloon business. She also urged him to give up drinking and gambling. Lewis did not change his habits, but he did sell his saloon. Adeline wanted him to concentrate on farming, but Lewis had other ideas. For months at a time he roamed the Indian country, swapping and selling horses.

Over the years Dalton babies arrived every year or so. In all, Adeline raised nine sons and four daughters. Two more babies died as infants.[1] With no land of their own, Adeline and her brood worked as sharecroppers.

In the late 1850s the Kansas-Missouri border region turned into a battleground. Proslavers and antislavers rode by night, burning and looting. In 1861 the Civil War brought new terrors. By then Lewis had moved his family to Kansas. The farm he started there lay eight miles north of what would become Coffeyville.[2] Somehow, the Daltons endured the long time of troubles. Adeline, Emmett said later, "was a stern umpire of our morals."[3] Her high standards kept Ben, Cole, Lelia, Lit, Frank, Eva, Leona, Nannie, and Sam in line. It was Grat, Bob, Bill, and Emmett who broke her heart.

With the war in full swing, Lewis tagged after the Union forces. At first he did odd jobs for the soldiers. Later, he bought half-wild horses from the Osage Indians and resold them to the army. With their father gone, the older boys worked on nearby farms. The money they brought home helped the Daltons survive.

Hardships or no, the family continued to grow. Frank had been born in 1859. Then came the four boys who grew up to be outlaws. Grat (short for Grattan) arrived in 1861. He grew up mean and hefty. Quick-witted Bill followed four years later. The Daltons always said he was the best talker in the family. Cool and handsome Bob was born in 1869. He grew up to be a blue-eyed, sandy-haired six-footer. In 1871 Adeline gave birth to Emmett. Smaller and darker than Bob,

Emmett had Grat's temper and Bill's sly tongue. The last children, twins Sam and Hannah, were born in 1879.[4]

The final shots of the Civil War were fired in 1865. When the army left, so did the market for Lewis's horses. To help out, Adeline's relatives gave the Daltons a small farm near Belton, Missouri. Everyone pitched in to build a house and a corral. For a time, Adeline was able to enjoy a normal home life. She played hymns on

James Lewis Dalton, Jr., (left) moved his family to a farm near Coffeyville, Kansas, during the Civil War. Red-haired Adeline Younger (right) married Lewis Dalton when she was only sixteen. In the hard years that followed, she tried to raise her children to be law-abiding citizens. The lessons rubbed off on nine of her children. Four of the boys, however, chose the outlaw trail.

her rickety piano. On Sundays she herded the children off to church. When Lewis went off to travel with a circus, the boys did the farm chores. In slack seasons they attended a one-room schoolhouse.

The return of peace inspired a new era of lawlessness. Gangs of ex-soldiers took up a new trade as bank and train robbers. Lewis liked to brag about knowing Frank and Jesse James. The boys loved to hear him talk about the outlaws and their daring exploits. None of this pleased Adeline. Her younger sons were growing up wild and reckless. She often took a switch to their backsides to punish them.[5]

Adeline had good reason to worry. At sixteen, Grat was a drunken bully. Bill was spending his spare time at the card tables. The locals said Frank, Bob, and Emmett were just plain mean. All five bragged that they were kin to the Younger brothers.

The world of the Dalton boys revolved around guns and horses. When he was twelve Emmett sold some coonskins and bought an old musket. Owning a gun allowed him to join his brothers in their daily shooting practice. Emmett swelled with pride the day he heard a U.S. marshal say, "That Dalton boy is going to be a tough man to handle when he gets growed up."[6]

3

FROM LAWMEN TO OUTLAWS

The Daltons were not through moving. In 1882 the family headed west to Oklahoma, which was then known as Indian Territory. Lewis took a lease on a piece of land in the Cherokee Nation. Young Emmett found work as a cowboy on the Bar X Bar Ranch. At the nearby Turkey Track Ranch he met Charlie Pierce, Bitter Creek Newcomb, and Charley Bryant. All three later rode with the Dalton gang.

Grat and Frank hired on with the Cherokee tribal police. Their job was to keep settlers from moving onto tribal lands. In 1884 Frank turned in his badge and Bob took his place. Stories that Bob and Grat could be bribed passed from mouth to mouth. Pay them enough, the story went, and they will look the other way.

Unlike his brothers, Frank took pride in serving as a lawman. He signed on as a deputy marshal for Isaac

Parker, the famous "Hanging Judge." True to his nickname, Parker sent many an outlaw to the gallows. Working out of Fort Smith, Arkansas, Frank earned $2.50 for each outlaw he caught.[1] For backup, Frank hired Grat to be his posseman. Grat rode with Frank and guarded his prisoners. Both men knew they were taking big risks. Almost a third of Judge Parker's marshals died in the line of duty.[2]

Selling whiskey to the Indians was a big—and illegal—business. In 1887 Frank and a deputy tracked down a gang of whiskey runners. The outlaws opened fire when they saw the lawmen. Frank went down, badly wounded. His deputy killed three of the gang.

Frank was the oldest of the Dalton brothers. When the family moved to Oklahoma Territory, he put on the star of a peace officer. Later he served as a deputy for Isaac Parker, the famous "hanging judge." A gang of whiskey runners killed Frank in an 1887 shootout.

By the time he was sixteen, Grat Dalton was well on the way to becoming a drunk and a bully. He liked to brag that he was kin to the train-robbing Younger brothers. Those who knew him were not surprised when he turned outlaw.

The fourth outlaw ended Frank's life with a second bullet, then made his escape.

Grat stepped up to take Frank's place. Bob rode along as his posseman. The job gave the boys a chance to practice a new scheme. The trick was to stop a wagon-load of settlers along the trail. While Bob questioned the drivers, Grat would hide some liquor in the wagon. A mile down the road, they would return to "find" the hidden whiskey. Faced with arrest, the luckless settlers were happy to get off with a stiff fine.[3]

A year later the Osage Nation hired Bob as head of its tribal police force. The twenty-year-old took command of a force of a dozen Osage. Young Emmett

These well-armed Choctaws were charged with keeping the peace on tribal lands. The Cherokee and Osage tribes made the mistake of hiring Grat and Bob Dalton to lead similar patrols. Both men spent more time stealing horses than they did pursuing lawbreakers.

became his posseman. The teenager thought life in the Osage town of Pawhuska was exciting. He loved to swagger down the main street, wearing his .45 pistol.[4]

Bob seldom put in a full day's work. He looked after his horses and courted his cousin, Minnie Johnson. In the fall of 1888, the fifteen-year-old girl ran off with a farmhand named Charley Montgomery. Weeks later, Charley tried to sneak into town to pick up his clothes. Bob caught him and put a rifle bullet in his neck. To cover up the crime, Bob claimed that Charley was a horse thief who had resisted arrest.[5] The town guessed that was a lie, but Bob kept his lawman's star.

Grat joined forces with Bob and Emmett in 1889. For a time the brothers had a good thing going. They commanded the Osage police, served as federal marshals, and led a horse-stealing ring. Word of their night-time raids soon spread. Urged to act by local merchants, the Osage refused to pay the brothers' salaries. All three quit the tribe's police force, but kept their federal jobs.

Bob's dead-eye shooting soon landed him in more hot water. The trouble started when Alex Cochran shot Marshal George Cox. The Daltons went looking for Cochran. A storekeeper pointed to a rider who was leaving town. After a brief chase, Bob shot the man from long range. It was fine shooting—at the wrong man. The body turned out to be that of Cochran's son.[6]

Trouble and the Daltons seemed to go hand in hand. Bob lost his post as marshal for taking bribes from whiskey runners. He explained that he took the money because the government owed him for travel expenses. The weak excuse did not save his job. Grat lost his marshal's badge about the same time. As a prank, Grat had shot an apple from a boy's head.

Bob and Grat might have found new jobs as lawmen. They might have homesteaded or hired out as cowboys. Instead, they went back to a career they knew all too well. They became full-time horse thieves.

4

A BUM RAP IN CALIFORNIA

In July of 1890 Grat, Bob, and Emmett stole seventeen horses and two mules. Leaving Grat to guard the herd, Bob and Emmett set off to arrange a sale. They tried Fort Smith, but the dealers turned them down. The word was out. Any horses sold by the Daltons were likely to have been stolen. The brothers had to drive the herd to Kansas to find a buyer.

The Daltons returned to Claremore, Oklahoma, and tried again. This time they stole from the Indians who lived in the area. A Cherokee named Bob Rogers missed his stolen ponies at once. He gathered a posse and followed the Daltons north to Kansas. Rogers and his men caught up with their quarry in Baxter Springs. The sight of the Cherokees sent the Daltons dashing for safety. Bob and Emmett escaped. Slow-thinking Grat managed to stumble into the pursuing posse. He escaped a hanging, but soon found himself in the Fort Smith jail.

Grat spent only a few weeks behind bars. The local paper reported that there was not enough proof to hold him. More likely, putting Grat on trial would have uncorked a major scandal. No one wanted to think a former marshal had turned horse thief.[1] Grat left Fort Smith late in 1890. It seemed like a good time to visit brother Bill in California.

In the meantime, Bob and Emmett were recruiting new gunmen. Bitter Creek Newcomb, Charley Bryant,

For Emmett, Grat, and Bob Dalton, selling stolen horses was a way of life. As word spread that they were horse thieves, buyers became harder to find. In order to sell their freshly branded horses, the brothers had to make the long ride to Kansas.

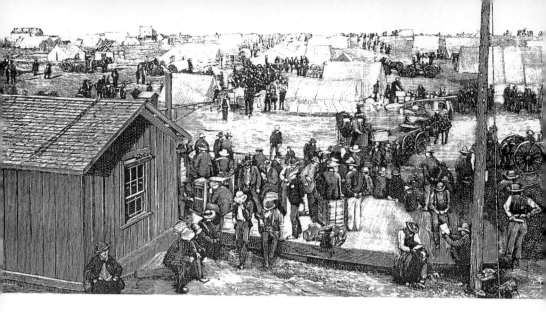

New towns sprang up along the railroad when settlers surged into Oklahoma in 1889. The Dalton brothers were familiar figures in tent cities like this one at Guthrie. Florence Quick, Bob Dalton's sweetheart, once talked her way out of the Guthrie jail.

and Bill McElhainie joined them. Bob led his gang to New Mexico, a territory known for its lawless ways. Better still, the town marshal in Silver City was an old friend. Marshal Ben Canty would warn them if he saw their names on arrest warrants.

The cost of living in Silver City soon emptied the gang's wallets. What to do? Honest work held no appeal. The Daltons decided to rob a gambling hall. The five outlaws sought out a seedy saloon in a small mining camp. As Bob had planned, they sat in on a card game. Even a tenderfoot could have seen that the game was crooked. The cheating gave the gang an excuse. They drew their pistols and cleared the tables of coins and banknotes. Then they backed out the door.[2]

A day later Bob happened to look back along the

trail. To his surprise, a seven-man posse was closing in on them. A few minutes later the posse opened fire. A bullet ricocheted and plugged Emmett in the arm. Bob led a charge that scattered the lawmen. The battle was won, but plans had to be changed. It seemed too risky to go straight to the hideout.

Bob and Bill McElhainie headed west to California. Emmett and Charley found work on a ranch southeast of Kingfisher, Oklahoma. Bitter Creek went back to his homestead near Guthrie, Oklahoma.

Out in Tulare, California, Bill was a rising young politician. He had been happy to see Grat. Now he welcomed Bob. All might have been well, but three men robbed a Southern Pacific train on February 6, 1891. The local grand jury blamed Bob and Emmett. Bill and Grat were named as their helpers.

Bob fled east without waiting for a trial. In July a jury found Grat guilty. A judge sentenced him to twenty years. While on his way to prison, Grat escaped and took to the hills. Bill was tried and found not guilty. He went back to his wife, but the arrest had ruined his hopes of a political career. Did Emmett and Bob take part in the robbery? Experts cannot agree. Some believe that Emmett was not in California that day.[3]

5

BIG RISK, SMALL PAYOFF

The arrests reinforced the Daltons' hatred of the railroads. Many common people shared their feelings. Railroad owners, they thought, were too rich, too greedy, and too powerful. To some poor farmers, outlaws who robbed trains were folk heroes.

In May 1891 Bob and Emmett set out to take their revenge. Charley Bryant and Bitter Creek Newcomb rode to Wharton, Oklahoma, with them. Thanks to Eugenia Moore, they knew the routine at the tiny whistle stop (since renamed Perry). Dressed as a man, she had pumped the express agent for information. The talkative fellow had told her what she wanted to know. At 10:30 P.M. on May 9, the Texas Express was due to stop at Wharton. The express car safe would be full of money on its way to banks in Guthrie.[1]

By 10:10 that night the gang was in place. Bob laid down the rules. There was to be no killing. The passengers must be left alone. Charley hated the second rule. He had been looking forward to emptying some wallets. Bob shut him up. "These are working folks like us and we don't steal from them," he said.[2] Playing by the rules would keep the local farmers on their side. As matters now stood, no one would help a posse find them.

Emmett and Charley took up their posts by the tracks. Bob and Bitter Creek strolled into the Wharton depot. The young station master went on with his duties. The sight of two dusty cowboys did not alarm him. No one in the station matched Bob's face with the reward poster tacked to the wall. Satisfied, the two outlaws moved outside to meet the train.

The Texas Express chugged into Wharton only two minutes late. As the train came to rest, Bob and Bitter Creek stepped forward. Two warning shots brought the engineer and fireman scrambling down from the cab. Emmett and Charley kept them covered. Back in the express car, the clerk heard the shots. Quickly, he began hiding money and valuables. The station agent doused all the lights in the depot.

Bob and Bitter Creek hopped into the express car. Bob ordered the clerk to open the safe. Loyal to his employer, the man said he did not know the combination. Thanks to his days as a marshal, Bob knew this was a lie. He fired a shot into the floor. The clerk's memory improved at once. He opened the safe and handed Bob a large package. Bob dropped it into a sack. Then he

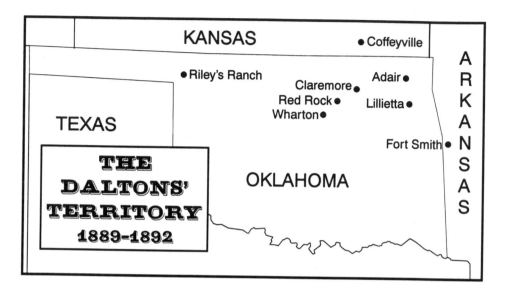

Except for short stays in New Mexico and California, the Daltons stayed close to their Oklahoma roots. Wharton, Lillietta, Red Rock, and Adair were the sites of successful train robberies. After each robbery they holed up at Riley's Ranch.

reached into the safe and grabbed a smaller package. That went into the sack, too. Outside, the passengers were starting to leave the train. A volley of shots from Emmett and Charley sent them back to their seats.

Certain he had cleaned out the express car, Bob gave the order to leave. The outlaws mounted their horses and spurred them forward. As they rode past the station, someone turned the lamps up again. The agent was hunched over his telegraph key, tapping out a plea for help. As to what happened next, the facts are hard to pin down. Some western writers say that Charley killed the agent with a single shot.[3] The local newspapers did not report a killing.[4]

Twenty miles out of town, the outlaws stopped to divide the loot. Bob ripped open the large bundle—and cursed. The package was stuffed with scraps of paper. The smaller bundle did contain about $1,600. For risking their lives, the men had earned only $400 each. A gambler could make that much in a good night. Later, the Daltons learned how they had been tricked. The clerk had hidden thousands of dollars in an empty stove.[5]

With posses on their trail, the gang went into hiding. Holed up on a remote ranch, they thought about the future. Except for the small payoff, the robbery had gone well. Bob began to plan bigger and better jobs.

Busy by day, the train station at Wharton, Oklahoma, was nearly deserted on the night of May 9, 1891. The Dalton gang was waiting in the shadows when the Texas Express chugged into the station. The well-executed holdup had only one flaw. The outlaws rode off with only a few hundred dollars.

6

THE RED ROCK ROBBERY

Out in California Grat had his own problems. He spent the winter of 1891 hiding in a cave. In the spring of 1892 he made the long trek home to Oklahoma. As soon as one horse wore out, he stole another. The 2,000-mile ride took 107 days.[1]

Bob and Emmett met Grat at a hideout in the Ozarks. Grat was annoyed to find he had missed both the Wharton and Lillietta jobs. Emmett thought Grat was too thin. He cooked huge meals meant to put some meat on his brother's bones. As the other gang members drifted in, talk turned to the future. Bill, his career in California ruined, had returned to Oklahoma. Soon he was buying and selling real estate in Kingfisher. As he went about his business, he gathered information to feed to his brothers. The gang did the riding and robbing. As Emmett put it, "We were Daltons together, one for all and all for one."[2]

Local lawmen heard rumors that Grat was back. They guessed that his return meant more trouble. The Southern Pacific and Wells Fargo had posted rewards for the capture of Bob and Emmett. Posses combed the

Dressed in his best suit, Bob Dalton sat for this portrait with pretty Eugenia Moore in 1889. The true love of Bob's life, though, was Florence Quick. The legendary Florence, who sometimes dressed in men's clothing, was as daring as any male member of the Dalton gang.

countryside without catching sight of their prey. Despite the manhunt, the gang struck again on June 1, 1892. Bill set up his alibi for the night's robbery by strolling into a Kingfisher hotel. Once inside he made a point of talking to Marshal Chris Madsen.

While Bill chatted, his brothers were sixty miles to the northeast. Riding with Bob, Grat, Emmett, and Bitter Creek were Bill Doolin, Dick Broadwell, Bill Powers, and Charlie Pierce. Charlie Bryant was six feet under. He had died as he had wished—in a blazing gun battle. The town of Red Rock was dark when the gang arrived. A few lightning flashes lit the sky. The gunmen fanned out along the Santa Fe railroad tracks.

Minutes later, the southbound train pulled into the station. The gang moved forward, then stopped at Emmett's signal. Something seemed wrong. All of the coaches were well lit—except for the coach behind the express car. Bob held the gang back. At last, business done, the train pulled out of the station.

The wait was almost too much for Grat. He was keyed up, anxious to show that he could rob trains, too. He accused Bob of "actin' like an old woman."[3] Just as he was building up a full head of steam, Bob told him to hush. A second train was chuffing along the tracks. Caution had paid off. The first train had been a trap. The dark coach had been full of armed guards.

Grat spurred his horse alongside the engine. Timing his leap, he swung up into the cab. At his orders, the engineer stopped the train. Back in the express car, the two clerks grabbed their rifles. They opened fire, driving the outlaws to cover. After a fifteen-minute battle, they gave up. The gang had them outgunned. Bob led two of his men into the express car. Despite the guns pointed at them, the clerks said they could not open the safe. One of the outlaws picked up a sledge hammer. One smashing blow opened the door.

After looting the safe, the outlaws tore into a shipment of clothing. Bob, Emmett, and Bitter Creek picked out dresses for their girlfriends. By ten o'clock, the gang had ridden into the darkness. Back in Kingfisher, Bill glanced at his pocket watch. Then he said goodnight and left the hotel. He knew he had an alibi that was as good as gold.

Emmett said later that the Red Rock raid netted nearly $11,000.[4] The express company put a much lower figure on its losses. Either way, no one in the gang could think of retiring after the loot was split nine ways. Money, however, was not the gang's chief worry. After three train robberies, the hunt was on in earnest. To elude pursuit, the gang scattered. Bob's training as a U.S. marshal was paying big dividends. He always seemed to know what the lawmen would do next.

7
"WE EXPECTED YOU FELLERS AT PRYOR CREEK"

More than a hundred lawmen joined the hunt for the Dalton gang. Cherokee tribal police supplied their tracking skills. One by one, the posses checked out the gang's known haunts. Friends of the outlaws had fun handing out false leads. One posse picked up a hot trail, but lost it in the Cimarron Hills near the Oklahoma-Kansas border. By June 17, 1892, all of the lawmen had given up the chase.

Legend tells us that the hunters did bag one trophy. It all started when a lawman discovered that Bob had been visiting his new girlfriend, Florence Quick. Alerted to the danger, the quick-witted Florence saw a chance to pull a fast one. Posing as a good citizen, she went to Marshal Ed Kelley. Bob would be coming to see her, she said. Florence then offered to let the marshal know the exact date. Dead or alive, I want the reward money as soon as Bob is taken, she added.

When the day came, Kelley showed up with three deputies. Florence pointed to her guest. "He's your man," she said. After the arrest, Marshal Madsen came by to see the prisoner. One look told him that Kelley had been tricked. The man confessed that Florence had offered him $500 to pretend to be Bob. When they did meet, Florence and Bob had a good laugh. The scheme

The Dalton gang returned to a dugout retreat like this one after each robbery. To pass the time, the outlaws played games, whittled, and planned future holdups. It was at the Riley Ranch dugout that Bob Dalton hatched his plan to rob the Coffeyville banks.

had worked well except for one slipup. The ruse had been exposed before she could pick up the reward.[1]

Bob and Emmett holed up in a dugout on Jim Riley's ranch. From time to time, hungry young men found their way there. Most wanted to join the Dalton gang. Bob gave them a meal and sent them on their way. The gang's roster was full, he said. He knew full well what had happened to Jesse James. Bob Ford, a new recruit, had shot Jesse in the back.

Money—or the lack of it—was a growing problem. Bill was talking again about running for office. Then as now, a politician had to spend money to win votes. Bob, Grat, Emmett, and Florence yearned to retire to a safe haven. One big jackpot might make it possible, they thought. To prepare the way, Florence made a scouting trip to Mexico. She found land for sale, but the owners wanted large down payments. Florence came back empty-handed.

What the Daltons lacked in cash they made up in pride. As Emmett put it, "Jesse James never did no better."[2] To solve the cash-flow problem, Bob planned a July 15 train robbery at Pryor Creek. On the morning of the robbery, a farmer chanced upon their camp. Bound by Bob's rules, the gang let him leave without harm. But what if he gave them away?

Thinking quickly, Bob changed the plan. That same night, the outlaws boarded the train at nearby Adair. The engineer looked surprised. "We expected you

The Daltons hoped to make outlaw history when they rode into Coffeyville on October 5, 1892. No one, not even Jesse James, had ever robbed two banks in the same day. Grat, Dick Broadwell, and Bill Powers were assigned to the Condon Bank (right). Bob and Emmett targeted the nearby First National Bank.

fellers at Pryor Creek," he said.[3] The four lawmen who served as train guards put up a stiff fight. They opened fire when the outlaws stepped onto the station platform. Once again the gang's luck held up. Their return fire put all four lawmen out of action with minor wounds. The town's doctors were not as fortunate. A stray bullet killed Dr. Goff. Another wounded Dr. Youngblood.[4] Unscratched, the eight gang members rode off with $17,000. It was the Dalton gang's best haul. It was also their last train robbery.

Marshal Madsen redoubled his efforts. Posing as friends of the Daltons, his deputies picked up useful clues. The $5,000 reward for the arrest of any gang member loosened tongues, too. Bill was running into a roadblock of another sort. He found that talking to him made people nervous.

On October 1, a prisoner in the Fort Smith jail gave Marshal Madsen a hot tip. The Daltons are going to rob two banks at Coffeyville, he warned. At first Madsen was inclined to scoff. No one, not even the James-Younger gang, had robbed two banks at once. Then came word that Bob Dalton had been seen in Coffeyville. Madsen quickly wired a warning. The town stockpiled guns and went on the alert.[5]

8

THE COFFEYVILLE DISASTER

Coffeyville waited for the Daltons. And waited. When the gang did not appear, the sense of urgency faded. The town marshal left his pistol behind when he patrolled the streets.[1]

The Daltons were taking their time. Hitting two banks at once meant splitting the gang. Bob assigned Grat, Dick Broadwell, and Bill Powers to the C. M. Condon Bank. He and Emmett set their sights on the First National. The plan called for the teams to reach Coffeyville early in the day. If they came later, patrons might have withdrawn some of the money.

The gang members broke camp early on October 5, 1892. All of the outlaws carried shiny new guns. At 9:30 A.M., they reined up their horses in the center of town. Union Street, Bob saw, was under repair. He led his men to a nearby alley, where they tied their horses. At this point the Dalton brothers put on their disguises—three sets of false whiskers. Grat, they agreed, looked like "an ancient pirate."[2]

At Bob's signal the gang split into teams and headed for the banks. That was the moment the plan began to collapse. Storekeeper Alex McKenna saw through the false whiskers. "There goes [sic] the Daltons!"[3] he shouted. Cyrus Lee took up the cry from his ice wagon.[4] Merchants hurried to hand out the guns they had stockpiled.

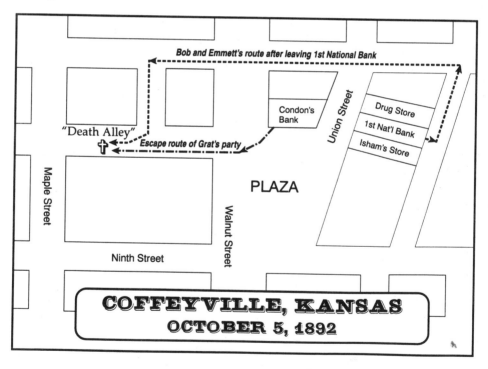

The Daltons were certain they had caught Coffeyville napping. Alert citizens, however, spread the word that the Daltons were robbing the town's banks. When the outlaws tried to escape, they had to run a gantlet of rifle fire.

If they heard the outcry, the outlaws ignored it. At the First National Bob ordered cashier Thomas Ayres to hand over all the money. Ayres took his time. The shouting outside told him help was on the way. He filled Bob's grain sack with gold and banknotes. When he started to add silver coins, Bob told him to stick to the "big stuff." After Ayres took some banknotes from the vault, Bob checked the vault for himself. He found another $5,000. The sack now held about $21,000.[5]

Bob and Emmett herded clerks and patrons ahead of them as they left. Heedless of the human shields, the waiting townsmen opened fire. The shooting drove the Daltons back into the bank. They stopped to return fire, then fled by the back door. In the alley they ran into Lucius Baldwin, a young store clerk. Bob took one look at Baldwin's pistol and shot him in the chest.

Emmett clutched the money sack as the brothers sprinted for their horses. The alley led them to Eighth Street, where they turned west. Firing as they ran, the Daltons gunned down bootmaker George Cubine. Old Charles Brown, also a bootmaker, picked up Cubine's rifle and opened fire. The outlaws shot him, too.[6]

Grat's team was having troubles of its own. After cleaning out the money tray, Grat had ordered cashier Charlie Ball to open the vault. Playing for time, Ball said the time lock would not open for ten minutes. Grat swallowed the lie. He said they could wait. Minutes later, rifle bullets shattered the bank's windows. Grat looked around for an escape route. Ball told him the bank did not have a back door. Again, Grat believed the lie. He untied the sack he had filled and grabbed a handful of banknotes. Then he led Broadwell and Powers through the front door.

Hidden marksmen blasted away as the outlaws emerged. Grat was hit, but he staggered on. Bob and Emmett met up with him in what later became known as "Death Alley." By some miracle, Powers and Broadwell reached their horses. Powers fell with a bullet in his heart as he tried to mount. Broadwell was wounded, but managed to reach the edge of town before he collapsed and died.[7]

Grat, growing weaker by the second, could still pull the trigger. One of his last shots killed Marshal Charles Connelly. Bob went down as a bullet found its mark. He struggled to his feet and staggered a few steps. A second bullet finished the job. By then Emmett had mounted his horse. Wounds in his arm and hip had not stopped him. Perhaps he could have escaped, but he turned back for his brother. As he tried to lift Bob onto his horse, barber Carey Seaman cut loose with his shotgun. A charge of buckshot spun Emmett out of his saddle.

In the sudden silence, someone yelled, "They are all down!"[8]

9

A NICHE IN WESTERN HISTORY

The Coffeyville raid was over. Years later, western writer James Horan would call it "one of the most idiotic ventures in outlaw history."[1] For now, Coffeyville stared in open-mouthed wonder at the dead outlaws. The bodies of Grat Dalton, Bob Dalton, and Bill Powers lay where they had fallen. Souvenir hunters ripped pieces of cloth from their shirts.

Rough hands carried Emmett to a room above Slosson's Drugstore. Dr. W. H. Wells called for two more doctors to help him. At one point a mob of angry men broke into the room. The leader said they were there to lynch the outlaw. Dr. Wells said not to bother, Emmett was sure to die. "Did you ever hear of a patient of mine getting well?" he added.[2]

Bank clerks counted the money picked up in the alley. The Condon Bank found it was short twenty dollars. The First National showed a slight profit. Bob and Emmett had walked out with $21,000. All of it came back, plus an extra $1.98.[3]

People poured into town to visit Death Alley. Many climbed the steps to Emmett's hotel room, hoping to see the famous outlaw. Preachers prayed for his soul. Rumors spread that Bill Dalton was forming a new gang. He's going to shoot up the town, the whispers said. Bill did come to town, but only to visit his brother. Adeline

Coffeyville took fierce pride in its victory over the Daltons. In this gory scene, townsfolk celebrate their triumph by showing off the bodies of Bob (left) and Grat (right). Bob's shirt has been ripped open by souvenir hunters.

came as well, to grieve over her son. By October 11 Emmett was well enough to move. The marshal transferred him to the county jail at Independence, Kansas.

Five months later Emmett went on trial. He pleaded guilty to second-degree murder, hoping for a sentence of ten to fifteen years. To his dismay, the judge sentenced him to life in prison. Emmett felt the judge had double-crossed him.

With the old gang shot to pieces, Bill Doolin stepped into Bob's shoes. Charley Pierce and Bitter Creek Newcomb joined the new Doolin gang. Bill Dalton also rode with Doolin for a while. A year later he formed his own gang and robbed a bank in Longview, Texas. In June 1894 a posse caught up with him at his ranch in Oklahoma. Bill was sitting on his front porch, playing with his daughter. When he reached for his rifle, Deputy Marshal Loss Hart shot him in the back.[4] How Florence Quick met her end is hard to pin down. Emmett says she died of cancer. Other writers say she died with her boots on and a six-gun smoking.[5]

Emmett was pardoned and released from prison in 1907. Fourteen years in the "iron corral" had reformed him. He married Julia Johnson and became active in his church. Two years later, he worked for a short time as a lawman in Tulsa.

In 1914 Emmett and Julia moved to Southern California. The Old West was becoming a favorite topic of filmmakers. Emmett, trading on his famous name,

Emmett Dalton was badly wounded in the shootout, but survived to stand trial. Sentenced to a long prison term, he emerged fourteen years later a changed man. Given a fresh start, Emmett married, moved to California, and starred in a film about the Dalton gang.

starred in a film called *Beyond the Law*. He claimed the film told the true story of the Dalton gang. In all, over a dozen films have tried to bring the Daltons to life on the screen. Critics say that Emmett's was the worst. After his brief film career, Emmett lectured, wrote books, and dabbled in real estate. He died in Los Angeles in 1937.

Of all the "bad Daltons," only Emmett lived to see the Old West die. He made a new life for himself, but he never forgot the old days. A reporter once asked him what he thought of the "modern badman." Emmett did not try to hide his contempt. "Why, I think the bandits we see today aren't worth the powder to blow 'em sky high with," he snapped.[6]

NOTES BY CHAPTER

Chapter 1

1. Harold Preece, *The Dalton Gang: End of an Outlaw Era* (New York: Hastings House Publishers, 1963), pp. 134-135. Emmett Dalton, in *When the Daltons Rode*, calls Florence by the name of Eugenia Moore.

2. Emmett Dalton, *When the Daltons Rode* (Garden City: NY: Doubleday, Doran & Co., 1931), p. 131.

3. Ibid., p. 133.

4. Preece, p. 138.

Chapter 2

1. James D. Horan, *The Authentic Wild West: The Outlaws* (New York: Crown Books, 1977), pp. 147, 149.

2. Harry S. Drago, *Outlaws on Horseback* (New York: Dodd, Mead & Co., 1964), p. 202.

3. James D. Horan and Paul Sann, *Pictorial History of the Wild West* (New York: Crown Publishers, 1954), p. 156.

4. Nancy B. Samuelson, *The Dalton Gang Story: Lawmen to Outlaws* (Eastford, CT: Shooting Star Press, 1992), p. 27ff.

5. Harold Preece, *The Dalton Gang: End of an Outlaw Era* (New York: Hastings House Publishers, 1963), p. 23.

6. Horan, p. 149.

Chapter 3

1. James D. Horan, *The Authentic Wild West: The Outlaws* (New York: Crown Books, 1977), p. 150.

2. Harold Preece, *The Dalton Gang: End of an Outlaw Era* (New York: Hastings House Publishers, 1963), p. 37.

3. Ibid., p. 39.

4. Emmett Dalton, *When the Daltons Rode* (Garden City, NY: Doubleday, Doran & Co., 1931), pp. 48-50.

5. Bill O'Neal, *Encyclopedia of Western Gunfighters* (Norman, OK: University of Oklahoma Press, 1979), pp. 81-82.

6. Preece, pp. 55-56.

Chapter 4

1. Harold Preece, *The Dalton Gang: End of an Outlaw Era* (New York: Hastings House Publishers, 1963), pp. 62-64.

2. Ibid., pp. 77-78.

3. Howard Lamar, ed., *The Reader's Encyclopedia of the American West* (New York: Thomas Y. Crowell, Co., 1977), p. 286.

Chapter 5

1. Harold Preece, *The Dalton Gang: End of an Outlaw Era* (New York: Hastings House Publishers, 1963), p. 104.

2. Jay Robert Nash, *Encyclopedia of World Crime*, Vol. II (Wilmette, IL: CrimeBooks, Inc., 1990), p. 860.

3. Harry S. Drago, *Outlaws on Horseback* (New York: Dodd, Mead & Co., 1964), p. 210; Preece, p. 108.

4. Nancy B. Samuelson, *The Dalton Gang Story: Lawmen to Outlaws* (Eastford, CT: Shooting Star Press, 1992), pp. 101-106.

5. *Fort Smith Elevator*, May 15, 1891, as quoted in Samuelson, p. 102.

Chapter 6

1. Frank F. Latta, *Dalton Gang Days* (Santa Cruz, CA: Bear State Books, 1976), p. 179.

2. Emmett Dalton, *When the Daltons Rode* (Garden City, NY: Doubleday, Doran & Co., 1931), p. 144.

3. Harold Preece, *The Dalton Gang: End of an Outlaw Era* (New York: Hastings House Publishers, 1963), p. 167.

4. Dalton, p. 149.

Chapter 7

1. Harold Preece, *The Dalton Gang: End of an Outlaw Era* (New York: Hastings House Publishers, 1963), pp. 182-185.

2. Quoted in Preece, p. 188.

3. Emmett Dalton, *When the Daltons Rode* (Garden City, NY: Doubleday, Doran & Co., 1931), p. 175.

4. Harry S. Drago, *Outlaws on Horseback* (New York: Dodd, Mead & Co., 1964), p. 219.

5. Dalton, p. 233.

Chapter 8

1. David Stewart Elliott, *Last Raid of the Daltons* (Freeport, NY: Books for Libraries Press, 1971), p. 26. This firsthand report was rushed into print soon after the Coffeyville raid took place.

2. Harold Preece, *The Dalton Gang: End of an Outlaw Era* (New York: Hastings House Publishers, 1963), p. 226.

3. *The Dalton Brothers and Their Astounding Career of Crime* by an Eye Witness (New York: Crown Publishers, 1977), p. 158. This is another hastily researched book written in 1892 to capitalize on public interest in the Coffeyville raid. "Eye Witness" is thought to have been a Chicago or Kansas newspaperman.

4. Preece, pp. 229-230.

5. James D. Horan and Paul Sann, *Pictorial History of the Wild West* (New York: Bonanza Books, 1954), p. 163.

6. Elliott, pp. 41-43.

7. Harry S. Drago, *Outlaws on Horseback* (New York: Dodd, Mead & Co., 1964), pp. 227-228.

8. Quoted in Horan and Sann, p. 164.

Chapter 9

1. James D. Horan, *The Authentic Wild West: The Outlaws* (New York: Crown Books, 1977), p. 151.

2. Harold Preece, *The Dalton Gang: End of an Outlaw Era* (New York: Hastings House Publishers, 1963), p. 256.

3. James D. Horan and Paul Sann, *Pictorial History of the Wild West* (New York: Bonanza Books, 1954), p. 162.

4. Bill O'Neal, *Encyclopedia of Western Gunfighters* (Norman, OK: University of Oklahoma Press, 1979), p. 88.

5. Preece, p. 275.

6. Quoted in Horan and Sann, p. 166.

GLOSSARY

Cherokee—A tribe of Native Americans who live in what is now Oklahoma.

Civil War—The war between the Northern and the Southern states, 1861–1865.

corral—A fenced area used for keeping horses and cattle.

express car—A special baggage car equipped to carry a train's cargo of mail, gold, cash, and other valuables.

greenbacks—A slang term for U.S. paper money.

Indian Territory—An area covering most of present-day Oklahoma that was once set aside for Native American tribes.

jury—A group of citizens sworn to judge the facts and give a verdict in a court case.

legend—A story that many people believe, but which is often untrue in whole or in part.

lynch mob—An out-of-control crowd that wants to hang someone.

MK&T—The Missouri, Kansas, and Texas Railroad, also known as the Katy.

Osage—A tribe of Native Americans who lived in what is now Oklahoma and Kansas during the period the Daltons were most active.

posse—A group of citizens who join with lawmen to help capture fleeing outlaws.

posseman—A guard or deputy hired to aid a U.S. marshal.

second-degree murder—The unlawful killing of another person, but without advance planning or intent.

sharecroppers—Farm families that worked someone else's land in return for a share of the crops they raised.

signal arm—A mechanical device used by railroads to tell oncoming trains to either stop or procede.

vault—The steel-walled strongroom where a bank keeps its money, bonds, and other valuables.

whistle stop—A slang term for a town so small that trains stop there only when signaled.

MORE GOOD READING ABOUT THE DALTON GANG

The Dalton Brothers and Their Astounding Career of Crime by an Eye Witness. Introduction by James D. Horan. New York: Crown Publishers, 1977. Original edition published 1892.

Dalton, Emmett. *When the Daltons Rode.* Garden City, NY: Doubleday, Doran & Co., 1931.

Drago, Harry S. *Outlaws on Horseback.* New York: Dodd, Mead & Co., 1964.

Elliott, David Stewart. *The Last Raid of the Daltons.* Freeport, NY: Books for Libraries Press, 1971. Original edition published 1892.

Horan, James D. *The Authentic Wild West: The Outlaws.* New York: Crown Publishers, 1977.

Horan, James D., and Paul Sann. *Pictorial History of the Wild West.* New York: Crown Publishers, 1954.

Latta, Frank F. *Dalton Gang Days.* Santa Cruz, CA: Bear State Books, 1976.

Nash, Jay Robert. *Encyclopedia of World Crime*, Vol. II. Wilmette, IL: CrimeBooks, 1990.

O'Neal, Bill. *Encyclopedia of Western Gunfighters.* Norman, OK: University of Oklahoma Press, 1979.

Preece, Harold. *The Dalton Gang: End of an Outlaw Era.* New York: Hastings House, 1963.

Samuelson, Nancy B. *The Dalton Gang Story: Lawmen to Outlaws.* Eastford, CT: Shooting Star Press, 1992.

INDEX